Cheltenham

OUTLINED · BY

AYLWIN SAMPSON

PORTICO PRESS • CHELTENHAM

All Saints church organ

Alstone Spa

Alma House

If the 200ft spire had been added to the unfinished tower as the architect John Middleton had intended, **All Saints' Church** would have been complete in its Victorian Gothic richness. Dating from 1868, its polished granite arcade, elaborate ironwork screen, and font cover, together with stained glass by Burne-Jones and two magnificent organ cases contribute to an interior that is breathtaking in its High Church character. There is a strong musical tradition too, for Gustav Holst's father was organist here and the boy played the violin as well as the trombone in small orchestras his father formed for special occasions. Perhaps most importantly Gustav made use of the organ for composing in 1891 Four Voluntaries for the instrument.

Until St James's Square was redeveloped, its west side could show neighbouring **Alstone Spa** as an example of the small spas which could be found distributed around the town. The wood kiosk had its pump, for dispensing waters, and was the final structure before house and annexe were swept away on Millbrook Street's reshaping in 2001.

One of Cheltenham's fine villas, **Alma House** in Rodney Road has a glorious interior. Its entrance hall has a grand staircase worthy of a London club, while the flanking room displays a copper-hooded fireplace beneath a romantic rural idyll of pipe playing and daisy-chain making in an Art Nouveau idiom. George Walton the Glaswegian designer was the originator of this opulence, while the local craftsmen of H H Martyn executed the work. The first owner of the house in 1835 was an Admiral Watts, but by 1878 occupants seemed to be mostly dentists. Later the Gloucestershire and Creamery company bought it in 1944 and lettings included such various enterprises as accountants, a fish restaurant, and 'This England' magazine.

A town which developed only two centuries ago is unlikely to have examples of medieval philanthropy in the shape of **Almshouses**. Nevertheless Cheltenham can produce one, even if its present location results from dubious dealing. For in 1578 Richard Pate provided for 'six needy persons' and a site in the High Street near Rodney Road was chosen. It was given a chapel, courtyard, orchard and 'each person ... a private chamber and garden'. Then in 1811 the land was sold for £250 to a Mr Smith who promptly resold it for £2,000. The needy persons were found a smaller plot in Albion Street, losing chapel, orchard and garden. That new home can still be seen sandwiched between later buildings.

The residents of the Hay Cottage Homes are more fortunate, for their picturesque accommodation looks out on the flowers and grass of Naunton Park. It was on the 80th birthday of Queen Victoria that the first stone was laid 'to provide for the aged and deserving poor without distinction of sect or religion', John Alexander Hay and his wife making their gift 'as a memorial of their long residence in Cheltenham'.

And in St Margaret's Road stands Dowty House, a former orphanage for boys, which in 1958 began a new life thanks to the generosity of many townspeople, including George Dowty. He gave £2,000 and encouraged his employees to make weekly contributions to help the thirty-seven old people resident there.

The history of a town can often be seen in its **Coat of Arms**. Cheltenham's shows two open books symbolizing the educational institutions, the cross of King Edward the Confessor, first recorded Lord of the Manor, a tree to signify the arcadian character of the garden town, while the pigeons are a reminder of their role in discovering the spa waters. The motto means Health and Education. Although the Arms were not granted until 1887, the town had achieved the status of a borough eleven years earlier, when Town Commissioners were replaced by a mayor and aldermen.

Pates Almshouses

the Borough Arms

Hay Cottage Homes

National Westminster bank, High Street

former County of Gloucester bank High Street

Miss Dorothea Beale

There are some fine examples of **Banks** in the High Street. At the junction with Rodney Road, on the site of the Assembly Rooms, is Lloyds, dating from 1900. Its architect was F. W. Waller who also designed the Town Hall in similar style. Nearby at the corner of Cambray Place, the Natwest building is worth study as a good example of 19th century conversion, while at the Promenade corner there is another instance of the heavy Baroque style so popular in Edwardian times. Originally it was the Worcester City and County Bank, as the heraldic shield on its façade will prove, though later it became the Midland. Also in the High Street, no. 147-51, the former C&A shop, and now 'Next', retains much of the appearance of the old County of Gloucester Bank, known as Pitt's Bank. In 1825 John Gardner, owner of the brewery and partner with Joseph Pitt in this bank, had to go hastily to London for money to avoid a 'run on the bank'. Then in 1888 the bank accepted £5,400 if the Borough Council would take responsibility for Pittville Pump Room and Gardens in settlement of Pitt's death debt of £10,800.

In Montpellier the spa's Rotunda had another branch of the Worcester City and County Bank in 1882, while the neighbouring Exchange on the site of Mawe and Tatlow's museum has been Barclay's premises.

In Clarence Street too, the former Cheltenham and Gloucestershire Bank can still be identified by the pair of niches with later sylph figures on its front.

Though not the first Principal of Cheltenham Ladies' College, it is **Dorothea Beale** who is remembered for its development. Her father was of Gloucester stock, based at Chalford; her mother of Huguenot ancestry. Dorothea was appointed Principal in 1858 and under her guidance the school prospered, gaining a reputation beyond the town. Under her leadership the move to new buildings in Montpellier Street took place in 1873, though bricks and mortar were not her only concern for she bequeathed her entire estate to the school at her death in 1906.

It was John Gardner, the banker, who founded a **Brewery** in the High Street in 1760. At his death his brother-in-law James Agg took over the concern, adopting the name Agg-Gardner. In 1858 his son, aged only 12, inherited, but it was not until 1888 that the firm became registered as Cheltenham Original Brewery. Despite a serious fire in 1897 the trade prospered, as is evidenced by the massive buildings dating from that time which can be seen along Henrietta Street. Since then various take-overs were made culminating in Whitbreads in 1963. Today the site awaits development.

Of other breweries little evidence remains, though in Winchcombe Street, at the Albion Street crossroads, Warwick Place still shows the last traces of Mr Pointer's establishment, with a wide arch, name panel and elaborate fanlight surviving.

'I am disordered by the Waters and diluted to the throat with medicine for the stone by **Dr Boisragon**' wrote Lord Byron from Cheltenham in 1812. This doctor lived at 11 Royal Crescent and his attendance on the Royal Family had earned him the title of Physician Extraordinary to the King, while the town's fashionable patients brought him a yearly income of £3,000. He was a prominent Mason, fervent Liberal and a leading member of the Literary Society, not forgetting his promotion of ballooning. His sons gained reputations in music: Theodore as a string player who pressed for a municipal orchestra in the town; Conrad as a singer at Covent Garden

At the corner of the High Street and St George's Place stands an odd building that predates its neighbours. Here one of Cheltenham's earliest guidebooks, 'Ruffs' was published in 1803, and six years later it saw the start of one of the town's newspapers, the 'Chronicle'. Subsequent uses included a pastry cook's, a jeans shop and now **Booth's Amusement Arcade** styled 'Casino Slots'.

Whitbread Flowers brewery

No 11 Royal Crescent

Booth's Amusement Arcade, High Street

Cavendish House

Brandon House

One of the caryatids between shops in Montpellier Walk

Charlton Kings: Hetton Lawn and Box Cottage

One of Cheltenham's most impressive villas, **Brandon House** stands at the corner of Painswick and Grafton Roads. It was built about 1825 for Henry Norwood Trye and its crisply carved stonework repays close attention. Inside, the staircase and rooms retain a distinction worthy of a past when, within the space of ten years, occupants included the Countess of Ponthieu, Archbishop Whately of Dublin and Admiral MacKellar. The grounds too were extensive, stretching to Tryes Road; today they are largely filled by newer houses.

'Clark and Debenhams' was the first of the Promenade's shops, but in 1883 it adopted the name **Cavendish House**, after the London square neighbouring the draper's business in Wigmore Street. The original 19th façade has been replaced by a severe design of 1964 and the management is now part of the House of Fraser group, yet its prominence and reputation continue to attract the shoppers, even if 'silks, muslins, shawls, gauzes, ribands, gloves, lace and fancy articles' are much changed in style.

In Montpellier walk there are 32 figures of armless ladies, supporting on their heads the lintels of shop fronts. Based on classical models at the Erechtheion in Athens, two of these **caryatids** date from the 1840s, the remainder are more recent. Two in fact were made only in 1970, but they are all important in adding charm to this area. Careful observation will reveal that their design is not wholly repetitive, for some have the right knee forward, others the left.

Charlton Kings has retained its identity even after incorporation into Cheltenham, not only through its medieval parish church, its varied architecture and distinctive estates like Battledown, but also by its rich literary associations. Two examples are Hetton Lawn where the grandparents of Alice Liddell lived, and Box Cottage in Bafford Lane the home of Cecil Day Lewis, the poet laureate.

In 1849 the foundation stone of St Paul's Training College was laid. The architect S W Daukes adopted an Oxford plan of quadrangle and entrance tower gateway in the Gothic style. Today the institution is part of the University of Gloucestershire and the site is known as **Francis Close Hall** campus in recognition of the role played by the forceful cleric in its inception.

Francis Close was instrumental too in the founding of **Cheltenham College**, the first Proprietary school in this country whereby parents bought shares giving them the right to nominate pupils. Opened in 1841, the College acquired a military reputation producing many who distinguished themselves in the army as well as others in the field of exploration. The buildings include a chapel, dating from 1896, that derives from King's College Cambridge, and Thirlestaine House, bought in 1947, thereby adding a classical composition to the Gothic main buildings.

Cheltenham Ladies' College , also founded on the proprietary system, dates from 1853 and, developing rapidly under Miss Beale, pioneered an innovative regime for the education of girls. Here the architect John Middleton adopted a robust Gothic/French style, but later additions have been widely varied architecturally.

The **Odeon cinema**, opened in 1933, is an interesting example of the buildings produced in the heyday of this form of entertainment. Live performances too featured such stars as Tommy Steele, the Beatles and the Goons.

As to be expected in a town that experienced a profound religious revival in the 19th centuries, Cheltenham can show a number of **nonconformist chapels**. Most are classical in their façades though many have today been converted to other uses. Fine examples can be seen in Clarence Parade and Cambray Place.

Francis Close Hall

Cheltenham College

Former Wesleyan chapel, St George's Street, and 'Highbury Chapel, Grosvenor Street

Figures on the Odeon cinema façade

Cheltenham Ladies' College

Revd Francis Close

Former Daffodil cinema

Claremont Lodge

'The great man of the place, monarch of all he surveys ... the pope of Cheltenham': such were the descriptions in the Reverend **Francis Close**. He came as curate of Holy Trinity church in 1824; he left as rector of the parish church in 1856, to become Dean of Carlisle. In the intervening years he preached powerfully against gambling, alcohol, theatres, tobacco, horse-racing, even railways running on Sundays. Politically a Conservative, Evangelical in churchmanship, he espoused the virtues of education. Infant schools, colleges and churches in the town owe their founding largely to him. 'Never did Beau Nash rule with more absolute supremacy. The authorities of the town sink into insignificance when their influence is placed beside that of the potent vicar'!

Francis Close would certainly have disapproved of the **Daffodil cinema**, which began showing films in 1922. Its style is hardly brash, with a chequered tile entrance and floral decoration that are redolent of the inter-war years. Now it has been converted into a restaurant; would this have earned his acquiescence?

For many admirers of Regency architecture **Claremont Lodge**, at the junction of Vittoria Walk and Montpellier Spa Road, ranks high. Interestingly the house's top floor was added later and the street front with its 'porthole' windows came into being only when the original front door and its courtyard were enclosed. Most intriguing of all, there is a depiction of the house in its initial form painted in the plaster over a fireplace. Outside even the pavement marks the entrance with a pattern. Not surprisingly there have been distinguished occupants: in 1837 Sir William Burdett, in 1845 the Revd Sir Nicholas Chinnery, and from 1919 to 1927 Dr James Clay Shaw an authority on insanity at Barts, who condemned women's participation in sport as marring their nature.

It is the contribution of squares that gives Cheltenham its 'garden-town' character and **Clarence Square,** named after the Duke of Clarence who became William IV, is a fine example. It was laid out in the late 1820s and the terraces bounding it date from 1832; that on the west side is not of classical style but Gothic. A notable resident at no. 19 was Charles Sturt the explorer of Australia. The south-east corner had been the site of a farmhouse called Field Lodge or Arkell's Farm and it was here in 1803 that the famous actress Sarah Siddons stayed, recovering from her 'anguish and selfish grief' after the death of her daughter, Sally

The six-house terrace of 1825 in Winchcombe Street known as **Columbia Place** was built as a speculative project by Thomas Thompson who had made his fortune supplying cavalry equipment to South America. In Colombia he added to his finances a monopoly for the refining and sale of salt. On a visit to take the waters in Cheltenham he decided to employ William Jay to design the building and the result was this somewhat idiosyncratic Greek style terrace which William Cobbett described as 'gaudy and fantastical'.

First class cricket has been played here since 1872 when James Lillywhite, coach at Cheltenham College, suggested a match should be played on its ground during the summer holiday. Its success, helped by the exploits of the county's captain, W G Grace, prompted further fixtures and by 1878 a second match was introduced, thereby creating a cricket week. Then in 1906 the addition of a third elevated the event to a **Cricket Festival**. There have been notable performances here, not least when in 1935 the home side beat the South African tourists by 83 runs and in 1979 when Yorkshire were humbled by a hat trick of lbw's, thereby echoing the Somerset match of 1893 when uniquely the home side achieved a hat trick of stumpings.

Clarence Square

Columbia Place

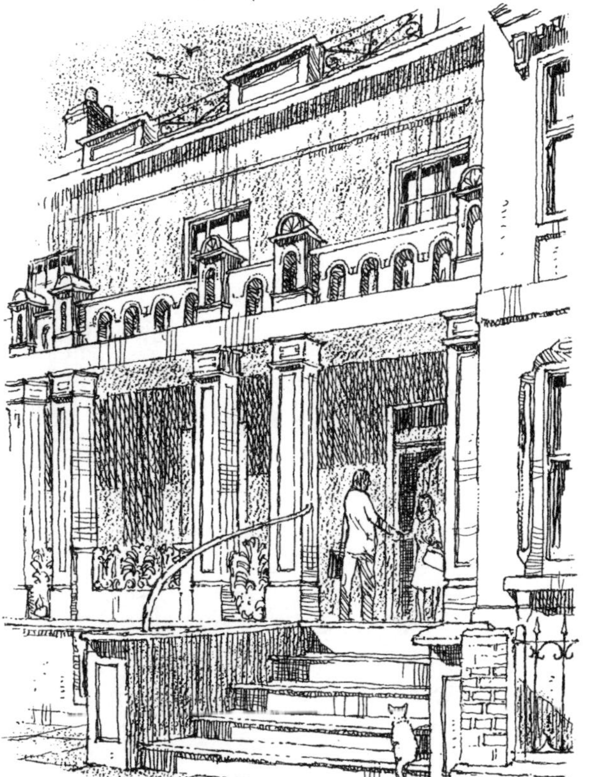

the Cricket Festival on Cheltenham College Ground

Sidney Lodge, former home of Baron de Ferrières

Pier at the Park surviving from Tudor Lodge, S.W. Daukes' house

Former Devonshire Street School

There have been many benefactors of Cheltenham, but foremost must be **Baron de Ferrières**. Born in 1823 in Utrecht he came to the town in 1860 and soon involved himself in its affairs. One of its first aldermen in 1876, he was made the borough's second mayor the following year and was elected to Parliament in 1880. His benefactions to churches and schools were generous, but perhaps his most notable gesture was the gift of forty-three paintings from his father's collection of 17th century Dutch and 19th century Belgian artists together with £1,000 towards the provision of an art gallery for the town. His house in Overton Road with its extraordinary stonework, now called Sidney Lodge, stands on the site of Lord Fauconberg's Bayshill House where another, more indirect benefactor, George III, stayed.

In 1839 **Samuel Whitfield Daukes** purchased The Park and, redeveloping it, decided to settle there, building to his own design his house Tudor Lodge. He was an architect who contributed many notable structures in Cheltenham and further afield: the Lansdown railway station, St Peter's church, Francis Close Hall, Cirencester Royal Agricultural College and St Saviour's, Tetbury. Sadly all that survives of his own home is a gate pier. He died at Beckenham, Kent, in 1880 and was buried in the family vault at Highgate cemetery. Incidentally, one grandson became a bishop and another one was knighted.

Devonshire Street School can claim a longer pedigree than many other of the private educational foundations in the town, for it was the direct successor to a school established in 1683 over the north porch of the parish church. Thanks to the support of Francis Close it relocated off the High Street when National Schools began, though its pupils may have missed playing in the churchyard or even manhandling their aged master, John Garn, up the steep stairs to the classroom.

'He has never yet received any lesson, pursues Latin, French by himself at intervals between business ... he remembers everything he devours', so his father noted. **Sydney Dobell** attended no school or university, yet proved a master of language, blameless in character and philanthropic to all. He championed struggling authors while identifying himself in his most notable poem 'The Roman' with the aspirations of Italian unity. He was praised by Mazzini, Tennyson, Carlyle and Rosetti, forming, whilst living at Coxhorne, Charlton Kings, the Society of the Friends of Italy. As one reviewer said of his work, 'He has made the Chelt as famous as the Tiber'. For Dobell was a Kentish man, a Gloucestershire poet and a possible Poet Laureate.

In the St Paul's area of the town, **Dunally House** stands out as a stranger amongst its terraced artisan neighbours. Originally called Woodbine Cottage, when the Irish Lord Dunally took it the name was changed. A few years before its erection the site was used for the town gibbet and in 1777 a body was brought here to be hung in chains. The crime which led to this is recounted on a memorial in the parish church: Katherine A'Court had been poisoned by her servant whom she had found in the act of stealing and he thus paid for his revenge. When both corpse and gibbet disappeared shortly afterwards there was yet another death - that of the young man who discovered the remains a few years later whilst digging nearby!

It was a request from a Japanese aircraft company for six undercarriage wheels which **George Dowty** had invented that started the world-wide hydraulics firm in 1931. He had been working for Gloster Aircraft Company, but as it was unable to meet this request, he resigned his position and rented a mews loft behind his flat in Lansdown. There he constructed by himself the order, despite a neighbouring petrol store with wood shavings below – and no fire insurance. The job was done within two months; the rest, as they say, is history.

Coxhorne, Charlton Kings, home of Sydney Dobell

Dunally House

George Dowty's workshop in Lansdown Terrace Lane mews

The auditorium of the Everyman Theatre

No 31, Montpellier Villas home of John Forbes

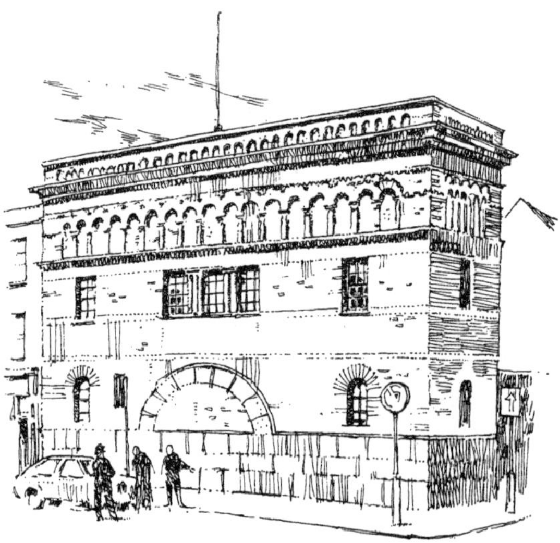

Electricity sub-station, Clarence Street

Originally The New Theatre and Opera House, one of the best examples of the work of architect Frank Matcham who also designed London's Palladium and Coliseum, it was built in six months. The reticent frontage to Regent Street belies an exuberant glittering interior. Opening in October 1891 when Lily Langtry, no stranger to the town, brought her company down from London, it has seen performances ranging from ballet to knockabout comedy, with such personalities as Ellen Terry, George Robey, John Gielgud, Margot Fonteyn and Robert Helpmann. From 1929 to 1936 films provided entertainment; the ensuing war encouraged stage productions, before television took away audiences. By June 1959 it had closed. But, thanks to local enthusiasts, it reopened a year later and became the town's professional theatre serving plays, ballet, opera and training programmes to local communities. Truly the **Everyman** has been a happy and appropriate name.

Designer of Pittville Pump Room, St Paul's church, as well as the Pittville estate, **John Forbes** was also a land speculator. Like many others he ran into debt and in 1834 forged a bill of exchange. Arrested at his home in Montpellier Villas, he was tried and sentenced to transportation for life. After a petition, this was commuted to two years imprisonment, though what subsequently happened to this gifted architect is unknown.

Based on the Strozzi Palace in Florence, the terracotta brick **electricity sub-station** in Clarence Street dates from 1895. The borough engineer, Joseph Hall, may have designed it, for he was responsible for the town's distinctive 'dragon and onion' street lamps. In 1907 it became offices and later a social club for the Electricity Company before returning to its original rôle. Incidentally, Hall later became Chief Engineer of Bombay, providing further links with the town's Indian connection.

One of Cheltenham's areas of small early 19th century housing, **Fairview** takes its name from a cottage which became the Fairview Inn. Many of the streets have still charming survivors of that time, an example being the canopied shop at the corner of Victoria Place.

Since 1855 there have been **Gas Works** buildings at the corner of Gloucester and Tewkesbury Roads. The offices are quite spectacular in their bright red brickwork, laid it is said by local apprentices from the Mechanics Training School. But the designer will have been a keen borrower from Gothic, French and perhaps other models, for it is a Victorian masterpiece of eclecticism.

The visit of **George III** to Cheltenham in 1788 was chronicled by newspapers of the time, not forgetting Fanny Burney's account as Second Mistress of the Robes to Queen Charlotte. Certainly the Royal Family's five weeks here drew fashionable society to the spa and helped to secure the town's development. But it also promoted the King's image as a man of the people by his freely mixing with the townsfolk , as well as his interests in the surrounding countryside's agricultural problems. When the royal party departed to Windsor 'all Cheltenham was drawn out into the High Street, the gentles on one side and the commons on the other,' as Fanny Burney wrote

One of Cheltenham's longest trading businesses was the **Gloucestershire Dairy and Creamery**. Founded in 1876, in Clarence Street the uniformed roundsmen drove pony traps painted red, white and blue up the Promenade to Montpellier. Five years later the firm moved to no 23 Promenade and provided an open air roof garden café. Then around 1928 the stables in Imperial Lane were acquired from Alma House and it was here that the firm stayed, till in 1993 it sold out to Express Dairy. Now there are flats where once there were floats.

Corner shop in Fairview

Gasworks offices

George III

Gloucs Dairy & Creamery, Imperial Lane

Gustav Holst

the Grammar School once in the High St.

Hoopers

Marie Hall

Gym Centre

Perhaps Cheltenham's most celebrated 'music son' **Gustav Holst** was as a child short-sighted and asthmatic, but his musical talent showed itself at an early age. When only four he quickly identified a tune his father was playing and later he took up the violin and trombone. A pupil at the Grammar School, his early compositions were performed here in the town and at the age of seventeen he was appointed organist at Wyck Rissington. After studying at the Royal College of Music, he taught in London, though he did return to Cheltenham to conduct his most famous work 'The Planets', seven years before his death in 1934.

Founded in 1578 by Richard Pate, the **Grammar School** was situated till 1965 in the High Street. It can number amongst its past pupils Frederick Handley Page the aircraft manufacturer, Benjamin Baker the constructor of the Forth Railway Bridge, Gilbert Jessop the cricketer and, of course, Holst.

One of the Promenade's impressive buildings, **Hooper's** first occupier in 1823 was Millet, an American artist. Subsequently called the Imperial Hotel, then by 1856 the Imperial Club 'for resident noblemen and gentlemen' it had within 20 years the more prosaic function of the town's main post office. But in 1987 another role change saw it become a prestigious shop.

The violinist **Marie Hall**, after her international career, settled in Eldorado Road in 1911, till her death in 1956. She gave the first performance of 'The Lark Ascending' which Vaughan Williams dedicated to her.

Although the **Gym Centre** in Montpellier Gardens has been demolished, the space it occupied remains as a reminder that here the audience sat to enjoy music from the 1895 bandstand, or the performances on the stage of the open-air theatre. Both these features survive, but not the seating with its reversible backs!

Like the Promenade, to one side of which it is attached, **Imperial Square** began life as part of the Walks and Rides of the Imperial Spa. Initially the centre of the square was used as a commercial nursery, as well as a pleasure ground for visitors to the spa and this role continues today with the profuse flower beds. During the 1830s terraced houses were built on north and east sides: but the south had to wait till 1996. Within the square a Winter Gardens glass structure of 1878 survived until World War II, while the Town Hall of 1903 still stands.

The small Regency House in Clarence Road, Pittville is now the **Holst Birthplace Museum** commemorating the life and work of the composer as well as preserving as example of the domestic furnishing in Victorian and Edwardian times, both 'below and above stairs'. Here can be seen Holst's own piano, memorabilia of his musical career, in authentic settings of kitchen, laundry, housekeeper's room, bedroom, nursery and sitting room.

Of Gloucestershire's notable cricketers, **Gilbert Jessop** has strong association with Cheltenham, being born in Cambray Place in 1874. Succeeding W G Grace as county captain in 1900, he made six centuries each in less than an hour, and when playing for England contributed 104 runs in 75 minutes at the Oval, after the side had lost five wickets for forty-eight runs. His nickname 'Croucher', his fine fielding and his fast bowling earned him a lasting reputation.

Built in 1849, the **General Hospital** was the successor to the High Street premises now called Normandy House. Over £2,000 was raised by townspeople to provide some ninety beds, though perhaps not so generous was the patients' diet of potatoes, bread, gruel and beer. Linen was changed but fortnightly and the regime somewhat strict, one surgeon insisting his patients stand at the foot of their beds, military fashion when he conducted his ward round. Today the newer extensions in pastel colours and modern style promise a less forbidding prospect in College Road.

Imperial Square

Holst's birthplace museum

Gilbert Jessop

General Hospital

Alpha House, Jenner's surgery

John Dower House

Joseph Pitt House

Jones Shoe shop

Leckhampton church

Although the town of Berkeley has most claim on **Edward Jenner**, being resident in Cheltenham from 1795 to 1815, acting as a Town Commissioner and helping to found the Literary Society might allow the spa some charge on this great benefactor. For it was whilst here that Jenner practised, at his surgery in St George's Road, vaccination against smallpox and moreover offered it free of any payment to the poor.

The presence of Royal Arms over the porch of **John Dower House** commemorates the visit in 1827 of the Duchess of Clarence. Not it should be added because she was required to appear at the magistrate's court, as it later became, but simply that Richard Liddell as landlord of a boarding house wanted to mark her short stay. Proudly, he even changed the name to the Clarence Hotel. Now the headquarters of the Countryside Agency, the use of John Dower's name perpetuates his great contribution to the establishment of National Parks in 1945.

Joseph Pitt House was called East Hayes in 1842, that is until the parishioners of Holy Trinity Church secretly raised £1,000 and bought it for their parson in recognition of his generosity in paying, for fourteen years, the choir out of his own pocket. Later the house became a boarding house and subsequently its name changed to that of the son of the developer of Pittville. Now once more changed, it is Lansdown House.

Originally known as Wight's theological library, **Jones shoe shop** in the Promenade has fortunately kept the appearance of its upper floors which would have been familiar to those 19th century seekers after spiritual reading.

The ancient church of **St Peter, Leckhampton**, though much restored, has a delightful setting. Inside its treasures include a Norman font, a vaulted sanctuary with an unusual room over it and the excellently preserved 14th century effigies of Sir John Giffard who lies moustached and equipped with sword, together with his attractive wife, in the south aisle.

Cheltenham's connections with **Leckhampton Hill** are strong, for some of the town's building stone came from it.. Commercial quarrying began in the 1790s with a railroad running down to the Malvern Inn in Leckhampton Road. Extended in 1810 to Cheltenham, a year later it joined up with the new horse-drawn tramroad to Gloucester, thus giving access to the city's docks. Quarrying has also given the hill its most distinctive feature, the so-called 'Devil's Chimney', an isolated stack almost certainly created when the incline railroad was cut. Finally, the hill has been immortalised in the opening lines of 'November Eves' by James Elroy Flecker, poet son of the first headmaster of Dean Close School.

From the 1860s to 1906 the firm of William **Letheren** produced fine ironwork for clients world wide. An example was the gateway to his own house in Cheltenham's Church Road, St Marks.

Another ironmaster who contributed so much to the legacy of the town's decorative ironwork was Richard Eede **Marshall**, who had an extensive foundry near St James's Square. Many railings and balconies can be identified as the work of Marshalls, if not by the founder, then by his nephew Charles who lived at Beech House in St James's Square.

One of the oldest businesses to retain its name, the firm of **Martin** can trace its present location back to 1841 when Samuel Martin moved from the High Street to Imperial Circus at the north end of the Promenade. With his son and a partner from France, the jewellers became known as Martin, Baskett and Martin. A branch was opened in Paris and in the 1850s a Royal Warrant granted as working goldsmiths, silversmiths, watchmakers and engravers to Queen Victoria. In 1890 George Dimmer, from Portsmouth, bought up the concern but kept the original name, as well as much of the premises' appearance both inside and out.

Leckhampton Hill

Doric House,
St Marks,
home of
William Letheren

Martins the jewellers shop

Beech House, former home
of Charles Marshall

H.H. Martyn's works at Sunningend, Lansdown

Spa Pharmacy, No 12 Montpellier Street, formerly Maskelyne's workplace

Milestone in Bath Road

The firm of **H H Martyn** was one of the most important in Cheltenham's industrial history, earning, over more than 50 years, an international reputation for workmanship in wood, stone, metals, plaster and stained glass. Coming from Worcester in 1866, Martyn first worked with the sculptor R L Boulton, then with E A Emms, a monumental mason. In 1908 he acquired Letheren's ironworks at Lansdown, renaming it Sunningend. Martyn's notable commissions include the Cenotaph in Whitehall, the Speaker's chair in the House of Commons and St Paul's Cathedral pulpit. Many ocean liners were fitted out, as well as palaces, banks and public buildings; locally churches and chapels display the firm's skill and in the field of aviation the Gloster Aircraft Company was established in 1917. Such wide-ranging activity ceased in 1971, though the name was resurrected in 1992 at Sunningend by another firm.

Born in 1839 **John Nevil Maskelyne**, the son of a saddler in White Hart Street, worked as a watchmaker at 12 Rotunda Terrace, Montpellier. But in 1865 he started a career that took him to London's Egyptian and St George's Halls where his skills as a magician brought fame Perhaps if back in Montpellier he had not been asked to repair a 'surgical appliance' which he identified as a medium's table rapper, he would never have developed his abilities to construct automata that are the envy of present day illusionists. But his inventiveness went beyond the stage, for he also created a variable spacing typewriter, a coin-operated lock, a ticket punch and interestingly a rare film of Queen Victoria's Diamond Jubilee.

Not strictly a **milestone**, for it is of iron, this survivor from the 1840s stands on the east side of Bath Road, by coincidence at no 184, for it has lost the last digit of its date. The reference to Market House is a reminder that this was once considered to be the centre of the town. Its location at the corner of Bennington Street is now marked by the plaque proclaiming Centre Stone.

One of Cheltenham's truly monumental buildings, the **Masonic Hall** presents an intimidating eyeless façade to Portland Street. Indeed, the panels above the niches are the only indication of its function for they display masonic symbols. Much of the interior furnishing dates from 1823, when it was opened, while the 1832 organ is the oldest in the town. G A Underwood, the architect, was himself a mason, so it is odd that he should have provided a side window that looks into the Temple, core of the secret rituals. Around the Temple walls panels list past officers, many well-known Cheltenham personalities like Skillicorne, de Ferrières and Boisragon.

A prominent feature of the Promenade is the large Portland stone 1893 **Neptune Fountain**, unveiled, according to a local report, 'with slight but sufficient ceremony'. It was designed by Joseph Hall, the Borough Engineer, influenced, it is said, by Rome's Trevi Fountain, and constructed by R L Boulton. It draws its water from the River Chelt running beneath.

Of the **mills** that stood along the course of the River Chelt, the most recognisable is that in Vernon Place off Bath Road. Known as Cheltenham or Cambray Mill, its more familiar name is Barrett's, after a 19th century owner. One of its functions was to divert water periodically for cleaning the streets: Edward Barthiam in 1561 had to three days a week and William Barrett in 1831 was ordered to 'permit water to flow as heretofore'. Another mill, Sandford, can trace its origins back to 1086, though the present structure dates only from the late 18th century.

The impressive terrace on the Promenade's west side has included since 1914 the **Municipal Offices**. Begun in the 1820s its architect may have been Underwood, and initially it was private houses. The exterior has in fact hardly changed, with a fine central portico and ironwork in abundance. Many a town would envy such a home for its Civic Fathers.

Masonic Hall

Neptune Fountain

Barrett's Mill

Municipal Offices

Scenes in Montpellier

Cheltenham's 'Continental Quarter', as it is often described, **Montpellier** has gained this reputation from its architectural character, its many cafes and bars, its speciality shops, as well as its name. Like other towns' fashionable areas it recalls the south France spa town of Montpellier where many British families were interned during the Napoleonic Wars. The founder of Cheltenham's Montpellier was Henry Thompson who bought the site in 1801, establishing the Spa, tree-lined walks and rides and Gardens. Soon small shops were opening as well as an opticians and a subscription library. Further purpose-built shops appeared during the 1830s and 40s, then in 1843 a block of shops known as the Montpellier Exchange, now Barclay's Bank, was built on the site of Mawe and Tatlow's Museum. By 1850 more shops in Old Well Lane renamed Montpellier Street catered for visitors, with luxury products like glass and china, together with high-class outfitters, the indispensable chemists and druggists and grocers that have continued till today.

One of the best preserved early 19th century examples, the Montpellier Arcade, still announces its identity with boldly carved letters. Dating from 1832 it was a complex of 16 shops, part of a project to create a new retail area, under cover and secured at night by gates. Amongst its specialities were a pastry cook, an artists' repository, coffee and cigar house and a jeweller. The Arcade was described shortly after its opening as 'though not extensive, yet presents a pleasing 'coup d'oeil' from the upper entrance ... lighted by a glazed roof'.

The most recent addition however is the £3 million Courtyard opened in 1985. With its twenty-two shops and restaurants surrounding a sunken piazza and glass-and-iron pavilion it has created a modern complement to the Arcade. The development also involved the continuation of the 1840s Rotunda Terrace in Montpellier Street by an almost undetectable fusion of old and new.

Where Ambrose Street branches off from the High Street, stands a building that has seen and experienced great changes. It was originally Segrave House, showing its connections with the Berkeley family. By 1839 an additional block was needed, for it had now become the town's General Hospital and space was required for twenty-bed wards as well as an operating theatre. Then ten years later medicine was succeeded by education, when it changed its name to St Mary's Hall, for women students of the Teachers' Training College. Another twenty years on and as Idmiston House it served as offices for the Inland Revenue and Department of Social Security. Now it meets the needs of holiday makers going to France and the name has changed again, to **Normandy House**.

In a town so thoroughly classical it is a relief to find examples of gothic. One such is **Oriel Lodge** in Oriel Road. Designed by Edward Jenkins, it was built in 1823 for Charles Timins, a retired sea captain who, it is said, brought back willow cuttings from the tree at Napoleon's temporary grave in St Helena. A later occupier of Oriel Lodge was Arabella Graham-Clarke, the favourite aunt of Elizabeth Barrett Browning. However the Timins family's associations persisted as late as 1931 when the great grand-daughter of Charles sold the house to the General Accident Insurance Company. Since then it has been offices for the Polytechnics Clearing House and Eagle Star Insurance.

Changes of name come to newspapers as well as buildings. In 1883 the 'Gloucestershire Echo' appeared on the streets calling itself the oldest in the country! In fact it had changed from the 'Cheltenham Evening Telegram'. Publication until 1891 was from 3 Promenade Place, but that year it took over Mr Hale's Piano, Harp and Music Rooms in **Promenade House**. There the 'Echo' stayed till 1996 when Yates Wine Lodge occupied the building.

Normandy House

Oriel Lodge

Promenade House

Regent House designed by Papworth

The Park

Playhouse Theatre

Pillar box in Bayshill Road

In terms of national reputation **John Buonarotti Papworth** was the most important architect to work in Cheltenham during the early 19th century even though some of his commissions were never carried out. Those which were include the Lansdown estate, the dome of Montpellier Spa and the reworking of Jenkins' St James's church. However it is Papworth's design for the Cheltenham standard villa that is most recognisable and its prototype was Regent House, 1825, at the south end of Vittoria Walk.

When Thomas Billings, a solicitor, bought the pear-shaped land in Leckhampton in 1831 he had ambitious plans for its development as Zoological, Botanical and Horticultural Gardens, exhibiting all manner of animals, landscape features and events. Despite a grand opening on Queen Victoria's Coronation Day in 1838, the enterprise failed and the property was sold to S W Daukes who converted it into a public pleasure ground, retaining a lake and broad avenue still known as the Elephant Walk. Since 1931 **the Park** has accommodated educational institutions and today is one campus of the University of Gloucestershire.

The buildings in Bath Road which offer amateur theatrical productions began in 1806 as Henry Thompson's Montpellier Baths with adjoining Salts Manufactory. Then in 1898 the Borough converted it into a swimming pool, but by 1945 the authorities decided to encourage amateur drama and converted it into a theatre. By 1957 municipal funding had been withdrawn, so the Theatre and Arts Club was formed and **the Playhouse** became the focus for dramatic and operatic societies. Outwardly the building has changed little and there are still the tiles at the bottom of the swimming pool underneath the auditorium!

Cheltenham has been fortunate in possessing eight out of only 94 in the whole country of the Victorian **Penfold hexagonal pillar boxes**. They are still in use and can be found distributed around the town. There are other Victorian and Edwardian examples too, allowing Cheltenham to style itself a pioneer of pillar boxes.

Cheltenham's largest and most ambitious Estate in the early 19th century, Pittville's acres are shown as a fine array of terraces and villas in **Pittville Lawn**. Stretching from the entrance gates at Winchcombe Street to the Lake, the roadway divides the Long Garden from the buildings. And what buildings they are: three terraces dating from 1826 to 1838 displaying classical Ionic columns and matching ironwork alternating with delightful villas in Greek, or in one instance Gothic, styles. The grandest example is Dorset Villa of 1840, home of the Whinyates, one of the town's leading military families.

The developer of this land, **Joseph Pitt**, was a local man who became a lawyer. Investing in banking, brewing and land, he was elected Member of Parliament for Cricklade in 1812. His Cheltenham acquisitions, apart from the Pittville land, included Church Meadow and the Marsh. On these, such developments as Royal Crescent and St Pauls were built. However, Pitt fell into debt and died in 1842 owing over £50,000, resulting in his entire estate being sold for the benefit of his many creditors.

It is the **Pittville Pump Room** that presents the visual climax to the Estate. Begun in 1825 to the design of John Forbes, the colonnaded exterior and sumptuous domed ballroom seem to evoke an age of Regency elegance. Unfortunately, fashionable society was attracted to the south of the town and the building became something of a white elephant; so in 1889 the Borough bought the Pump Room enabling later restoration in 1949 to return the building to its original state.

The gardens of Pittville have provided an example of the fashion for picturesque arcadia and the **Lake** with its bridges was formed by damming the Wymans Brook, making it large enough in 1866 to accommodate the launch of a lifeboat!

Pittville Lawn

Joseph Pitt

Pittville Pump Room

Pittville Lake

Linden Cottage, Prestbury

Bath Tavern and Bell Inn

Paragon Parade

The Queens Hotel

Perhaps the most distinctive of Cheltenham's neighbouring villages, **Prestbury** became part of the borough in 1991. It has a medieval church and in its most attractive street, the Burgage, a rich variety of houses. Some are half timbered, like **Linden Cottage**, others are of stone. They range in age through many centuries from the time when Prestbury was a small town and this was the old Market Place. Horse racing has been closely associated with Prestbury Park and the famous jockey Fred Archer grew up at the King's Arms.

Now known simply as 114 to 136 Bath Road, **Paragon Parade** with its distinctive early 19th century lamp holders was home to the novelist Anthony Trollope in 1853 during his career as a Post Office surveyor, and ten years later to Duncan Boyes who, as a midshipman, won the Victoria Cross but committed suicide aged twenty-three following a court martial.

Cheltenham at one time had a multitude of inns and brewhouses in its High Street. Many have disappeared, but enough remain in it and other streets as a reminder of those days: the Coopers Arms, High Street; St James Hotel, Ambrose Street; the Beehive, Montpellier Villas; the Exmouth Arms, Bath Road. Next-door pubs included the Compasses Inn and Welsh Harp in New Street and the **Bath Tavern and Bell Inn** in Bath Road.

Since 1838 the Promenade has had as its southern focus the **Queens Hotel**. Designed by the Jerrad brothers, it offered seventy bedrooms, twenty-five sitting rooms, coffee and billiard rooms, as well as a boarding house. Many guests of distinction in all walks of life have been here: royalty, explorers, authors, musicians, generals, politicians, actors – the list is long. Outside the entrance there is the surviving plinth of a pair which once carried guns captured at Sebastopol. They were sacrificed for the 'salvage drives' in the last war, but fortunately on the east side of the hotel two lamp standards have remained as reminders of 19th century private lighting.

There is only one reminder of the railway boom in the 19th century so far as stations are concerned in the town and that is a somewhat reduced structure. For **Cheltenham Spa Railway Station** lost its impressive columns and portico in 1961, though much of the ironwork supporting the bridge across the tracks dates from the original construction in 1840, while that for the platform canopy is some years later. However, vestiges of embankments, cuttings and railings associated with lines other than the Midland can be seen in the town. There is even a wall which marked the locomotive turntable in St James's Square where the GWR station, being a terminus, needed this facility.

In the High Street, at no 252, there is a façade that prominently displays **St George's Hall**. Opened in 1856 as a place for functions not large enough for use of the Town Hall in Regent Street, its first event was an exhibition described as a working model of the Crimea. Since then the Hall has hosted a wide range of activities. In the 1930s there were Red Cross training classes; in the 1960s previews of sculptures destined for the Montreal Expo. The Plymouth Brethren used it for worship in the 1940s, just as the Anglicans had 70 years earlier while St Matthew's church was being built.

Reputedly the most haunted house in Cheltenham, **St Anne's**, near All Saints' Church was built for Henry Swinhoe in 1860. He degenerated into an alcoholic, leading his second wife, Imogen, the same way. After the couple died, sightings of a tall woman dressed as a widow were reported, and for the next decade when the Despard family lived there she appeared both in the house and garden so frequently that the children played unconcernedly around her.

Cheltenham Spa railway station

St George's Hall,
High Street

St Anne's,
Pittville
Circus Road

Wynnstay House, formerly St James's Square Infants School

St Paul's church

St Mary's church

St James's Square Infants School was opened in July 1830, through the efforts of the educational pioneer Samuel Wilderspin, and Francis Close. It is the oldest surviving building of its kind in the country. The 60ft schoolroom has been extended but the tall windows are original and the playground, one of the first to be provided with swings, can still be identified, even if the ladies of Cheltenham no longer come to watch children at play. For some years the building served as a postal sorting office and then a printers. Now it is called Wynnstay House.

Designed in 1827 by John Forbes for the artisan congregation of this area, **St Paul's Church** has a classical front with a cupola tower and more modest brick sides in keeping with its rôle as a 'free church' where seats were without rental. Interestingly its wrought iron pulpit is movable by chain and runners. The church looks down St Paul's Street North off-centre because the field boundary dictated the alignment.

The oldest building in the town, **St Mary's Church** has much of Cheltenham's history in its walls. It dates from the 12th century with the central tower arches and has something of each succeeding century. The beautiful circular rose-window's tilting tracery, the flowing designs of other 14th century windows, the fine canopied piscina and the examples of the rich stained glass are but some of the treasures this, the parish church, has to show. Add to these the remarkable epitaph of Captain Henry Skillicorne, the memorials to Katherine a'Court, Sir William Myers, John English, William Grevil and many others, all of which contribute to St Mary's as a record of the town's life. Even the churchyard, with its preaching cross and brass measuring marks on the path, has something to offer despite the loss of many of its gravestones.

There are few original shop fronts in the Promenade, so it is rewarding to find an example that is virtually unchanged. **Scott Cooper** has been a jewellers since 1912, its 'art nouveau' decoration being a feature of the window frame and entrance door.

Apart from those in churches, examples of **sculpture** are to be found in Cheltenham's streets and parks. Taking statues first, Edward Wilson the explorer has his in the Promenade as does the Boer War soldier; Montpellier has Edward VII dressed informally, while Montpellier shows William IV in his Garter robes. The Ladies' College front on St George's Road is decorated by the figure of Hope with her anchor, the Neptune Fountain in the Promenade being a further allegorical subject. And on the parapet of the Pump Room, Aesculapius, Hygeia and Hippocrates stand sentinel. A modern sculptress, Barbara Hepworth, is represented by her abstract panels 'Theme and Variations' in Clarence Street.

Henry Skillicorne has his bas-relief in Imperial Square garden, but his memorial is the town itself. Indeed it was this retired sea captain who developed the spa, laid out the first walks and for twenty-five years supervised the 'improvements' that led to George III's visit in 1788. His achievements, extolled at length in his epitaph in St Mary's Church, make edifying reading.

It is its **Spas** which have given Cheltenham its character and expansion from small market town. The oldest spa building to be seen today is in Vittoria Walk where, at Hygeia House, Henry Thompson opened a supply of waters in 1804. Five years later another source was developed in Montpellier, the wooden pavilion there being succeeded in 1817 by the stone colonnaded building, whose dome was added in 1826. Of other spas, Imperial gave place to the Queen's Hotel, Cambray to a car park, Alstone to a shopping centre, leaving Pittville's Pump Room as the splendid survivor, still dispensing the Waters.

Scott·Cooper

Sculpture

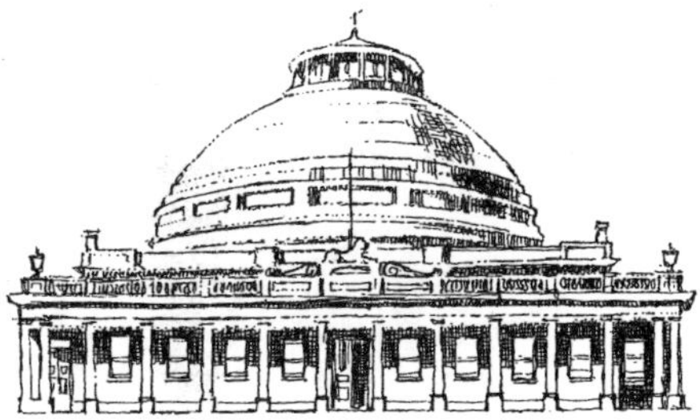

Henry Skillicorne

Former Spas: Montpellier and in Vittoria Walk

Synagogue

Charles Sturt

Street light standards near the Queens Hotel

Former antique shop in Montpellier Avenue owned by Ron Summerfield

One of Cheltenham's hidden treasures, the **Synagogue** can be found off St James's Square. Designed by local architect W H Knight, it is virtually unaltered since 1839. Internally lit by a roof light, the wooden furnishing probably came from a demolished synagogue in London's Leadenhall Street.

Army officer in Spain, France and Ireland, Surveyor-General of South Australia, Colonial Secretary to Sir Ralph Darling, Governor of New South Wales, **Charles Sturt** returned to England in 1853, his work as one of Australia's great explorers completed. Living for a while in Tivoli Road, he moved to 19 Clarence Square where he died in 1869 sadly before his knighthood could be accorded. Tributes followed, not only to his exploits and his skills in drawing birds and animals, but also to his personal qualities which we are told 'enabled him to pursue among savages a path never stained by bloodshed'.

On 28 September 1818 Cheltenham enjoyed for the first time street gas lighting and still possesses some attractive examples of **street lighting**. The earliest are the three oil lamp holders of about 1823 outside Paragon Parade in Bath Road and those two standards next to the Queen's Hotel are not much later. Then there are the 1887 'Gordon Lamp' erected in Montpellier commemorating General Gordon's death at Khartoum, and familiar 'dragon and onion' standards, designed by a Borough Engineer, Joseph Hall, which can be seen in St Mary's churchyard, Regent Street, Crescent Place and Trafalgar Street.

Among Cheltenham's many antique shops, that of **Ron Summerfield** acquired a reputation as much for its diversity as his eccentric personality. A passionate collector, he rarely sold anything except to finance further purchases and his house in Bayshill as well as the shop in Montpellier were renowned for their abundant contents. After his death in 1989 his stock was auctioned in 14,000 lots, took 25 days and raised nearly £8 million, the proceeds forming a charitable trust.

In 1820 the Earl of Suffolk sold land to James Fisher who, four years later, laid out what we now know as **Suffolk Square**. He employed local architect Edward Jenkins to design its terraces though progress in actually building them was slow. It was not until 1848 that the north side was complete. At the north east corner stands St James's Church which Jenkins had problems in roofing, while on the south side no 20 was the home of the more successful architect, Sir Robert Smirke. In the centre a bowling green, on what was called Horne Field, was laid in 1920.

Incorporated into the Borough in 1991, **Swindon Village** has a church possessing a rare 12th century hexagonal tower and next to it a small half-timbered cottage traditionally the home of Maud Bowen. She reputedly committed suicide and the elm stake planted in her grave eventually grew to 80 ft, being known as Maud's Elm. In 1907 it was struck by lightning and had to be cut down for safety but its location in Swindon Road can still be identified in maps.

Cheltenham's association with **Tennyson** extended over six years. When the family moved here from Kent in 1843 they lodged in Belle Vue Place, High Street, before taking 10, St James's Square. It was at the latter residence that parts of 'In Memoriam' were written.

Not to be confused with Thirlestaine House which is now part of Cheltenham College, **Thirlestaine Hall** stands at the eastern end of the road which takes its name from the two buildings. Built in the mid-19th century, its conspicuous dome was added in 1909 when a John Player, owner of a South Wales tin foundry, decided to pursue his hobby of astronomy with an observatory. His death in 1931 led to the house becoming deserted for eight years, to be re-used as an hotel, then the U.S. Army, followed by Royal Insurance till finally in 1973 the Chelsea Building Society.

Suffolk Square

Swindon Village

Tennyson's house, St James Square

Thirlestaine Hall

Houses in Tivoli Road

Called 'prestigious' by estate agents, 'a particularly attractive environment' by a Department of the Environment inspector, 'fashionable' by 19th century guide book writers, **Tivoli Road** is arguably one of Cheltenham's most engaging thoroughfares by virtue of its ambience, architecture and history. Laid out partially in the 1830s on land called Marybone Park, it was extended later to join up with the Park. Understandably the arcadian character was derived from the latter and many fine trees were soon to be found, not on the road side but in front gardens: beech, willow, Scots pine, Wellingtonia, Monterey cypress and cedar. Inevitably some have succumbed to storm or disease, yet there remain enough to preserve the streetscape's 'rus in urbe'.

The houses too have variety in style and age, from Regency villas ranging in scale from grand to cottage owing their façades to Papworth's design, Gothick fantasy, Tyrolean, Arts and Crafts, modern suburban or neo-Georgian. There are charming examples of ironwork, classical porches and imposing gate piers. Perhaps most intriguing though are the evidences of large gardens being infilled by later houses, of mews being converted to dwellings and of a former nursery still identifiable by the deep front gardens of the houses.

Above all it is the human history that is captivating: soldiers, surgeons, academics, musicians, actors, scientists, aristocrats - the list could go on. The explorer Charles Sturt, the diplomat Sir Peter Scarlett, actor Sir Ralph Richardson, a Mitford, nursing pioneer Dame Sidney Browne, Princess Imeretinsky, Oxford professor Hume-Rothery, all these are examples of occupants. Add to these visitors like Field Marshal Lord Birdwood and, perhaps, to show another aspect, two lodgers who robbed Cavendish House department store, inadvertently leaving a toe-print, their subsequent conviction being the first in this country through this evidence, and Tivoli Road certainly has had a rich and varied history!

Standing on the site of a nursery garden, next to the tramway from Leckhampton quarries, **St John's Lodge, Tivoli Circus** faces westwards along the A40. In 1853 the scene would have been much quieter for Prince Caulker who had been brought there by the Countess of Huntingdon's Missionary Society. But his six years stay was anything but happy, for in that time he lost his father King of Bompey, West Africa, his mother and his right to the throne. Added to these misfortunes, he also became blind.

Varied in its surrounding houses, **Wellington Square** has in its south west corner what was called a Botanical Garden. Established by Richard Ware in 1830 who also rented the Nursery in Imperial Square, it proved to be a financial disaster after his death two years later. Yet his layouts for landscaping Pittville warrant calling him 'Capability' Ware. On the west side, at no. 6, the actor William Macready enjoyed his retirement and entertained his friend Charles Dickens when he came to give his popular Readings at Cheltenham's Assembly Rooms in the High Street.

Perhaps the most impressive medieval house in the Borough is **Leckhampton Court**. Dating from the 14th century it has undergone many alterations and additions since, but the surprising thing is that over the 600 years only three families have owned it: the Giffard, the Norwood and the Trye. However, changes of use have been more frequent: Red Cross Hospital in the First World War; private school; rehabilitation of prisoners-of-war after the second; Sue Ryder care home since 1977.

The **Beaufort Arms, London Road** is a reminder that however choked with traffic the A40 is today, travel before the introduction of toll or turnpike must have been equally unpleasant. Payment of a charge which contributed to the maintenance of the stretch of road meant establishing toll house and gate. All have disappeared in Cheltenham but the one which existed on London Road has an echo in the inn with its bay projection nearby.

St John's Lodge, Tivoli Circus

Wellington Square

Leckhampton Court

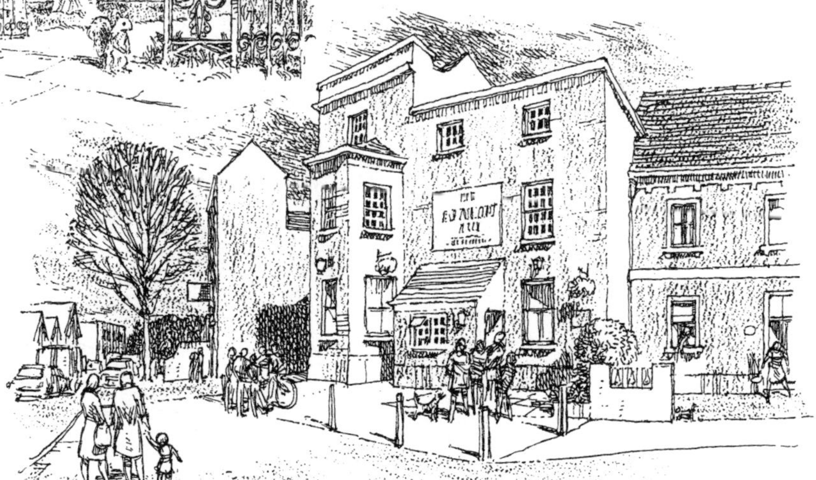

Former turnpike at the Beaufort Arms, London Road

Well Walk

Statue of
Edward Wilson
in the Promenade

Wilson's boyhood
home at
The Crippets

A tree-lined avenue laid out by Henry Skillicorne in 1738 began at his spa, crossed northwards over the river Chelt, through Church Meadow, now known as Royal Crescent, along the line of Crescent Place and arrived at St Mary's churchyard. Frequented by fashionable society for a century, with the rapid developing of Bayshill, Royal Well and the Ladies' College area its survival was no longer assured and today it is only **Well Walk** that serves as a reminder.

Artist, expert naturalist and, like his father, a physician, **Edward Wilson** was born in Cheltenham's Montpellier Terrace in 1872. Its identification is easily established for the details are incised on the façade. After a boyhood at Cheltenham College and at the Crippets up in the hills above Leckhampton where his love of nature developed, Wilson read medicine at Cambridge.

Chosen to serve as second medical officer, vertebrate zoologist and artist on Scott's expedition in 'Discovery' 1901-4, he produced many fine watercolours of Antarctica. Then in 1910 on the ill-fated 'Terra Nova' expedition he was Scott's Chief of Scientific Staff, being one of the five explorers to reach the South Pole. Their disappointment at not being the first there, the return in blizzard and sickness was the final tragedy ending with their freezing to death only eleven miles from safety.

The statue of Wilson stands in the Promenade, sculpted by Scott's widow, and a gallery commemorating his life in the town Art Gallery and Museum together with the memorial in Leckhampton churchyard are reminders of one of Cheltenham's most illustrious sons.

ACKNOWLEDGEMENTS

The success of *'A Cheltenham Companion'* has prompted this up-dated abridgement. Steven Blake, my co-author in that publication, has kindly checked the text and Jill Barlow has expertly prepared it for printing.

All three of us are founder members of Cheltenham Local History Society which, in its twenty-first year, will benefit from sales of this publication.

A.S.

Portico Press 33A Tivoli Road Cheltenham